AIR FORCE
SPECIAL OPERATIONS

Simon Rose

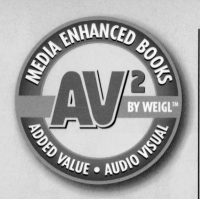

MEDIA ENHANCED BOOKS
AV²
BY WEIGL™
ADDED VALUE • AUDIO VISUAL

AV² provides enriched content that supplements and complements this book. Weigl's AV² books strive to create inspired learning and engage young minds in a total learning experience.

Your AV² Media Enhanced books come alive with...

Audio
Listen to sections of the book read aloud.

Key Words
Study vocabulary, and complete a matching word activity.

Video
Watch informative video clips.

Quizzes
Test your knowledge.

Go to **www.av2books.com,** and enter this book's unique code.

BOOK CODE

W463705

Embedded Weblinks
Gain additional information for research.

Slide Show
View images and captions, and prepare a presentation.

AV² by Weigl brings you media enhanced books that support active learning.

Try This!
Complete activities and hands-on experiments.

... and much, much more!

Published by AV² by Weigl
350 5th Avenue, 59th Floor
New York, NY 10118
Website: www.av2books.com   www.weigl.com

Library of Congress Cataloging-in-Publication Data
Rose, Simon, 1961-
Air Force special operations / Simon Rose.
    pages cm. -- (US Armed Forces)
Includes index.
Audience: Grades 4-6.
ISBN 978-1-62127-448-3 (hbk. : alk. paper) -- ISBN 978-1-62127-454-4 (pbk. : alk. paper)
1. United States. Air Force--Juvenile literature. 2. Special operations (Military science)--Juvenile literature.
3. Special forces (Military science)--United States--Juvenile literature. I. Title.
UG633.R672 2014
356'.16--dc23
                    2012043983

Printed in the United States of America in North Mankato, Minnesota
1 2 3 4 5 6 7 8 9   17 16 15 14 13

022013
WEP301112

Project Coordinator: Aaron Carr
Designer: Mandy Christiansen

Photo Credits
The photos used in this book are model-released stock images. They are meant to serve as accurate representations of U.S. Special Operations personnel, even though the people in the photos may not be special operators. Weigl acknowledges Getty Images, iStockphoto, Dreamstime, Alamy, and the U.S. Department of Defense as the primary image suppliers for this book.

Every reasonable effort has been made to trace ownership and to obtain permission to reprint copyright material. The publisher would be pleased to have any errors or omissions brought to their attention so that they may be corrected in subsequent printings.

CONTENTS

WHAT ARE AIR FORCE SPECIAL OPERATIONS?

Air Force Special Operations forces are units of the U.S. Air Force that carry out especially difficult missions. These units carry out their missions mainly from the air using a variety of aircraft. Some personnel, such as combat controllers, work on the ground to support air missions. Others perform search and rescue or **reconnaissance** missions.

Air Force Special Operations forces are part of the Air Force Special Operations Command (AFSOC). AFSOC is a division of the United States Special Operations Command (USSOCOM), which includes all of the special forces for the various branches of the U.S. military. The Department of Defense is in charge of the USSOCOM and all branches of the Armed Forces, except the Coast Guard. AFSOC has about 15,000 personnel. This includes those on active duty, those in the **Air National Guard** and **Air Force Reserve**, and **civilian** employees.

★ Air Force Special Operations teams may carry out combat missions on the ground to prepare the way for air attacks.

USSOCOM Organizational Structure

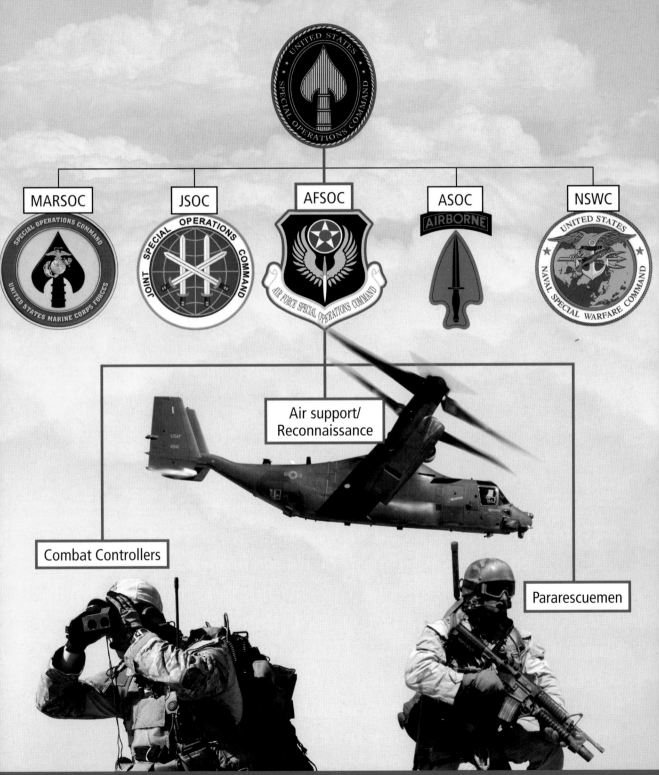

MARSOC

JSOC

AFSOC

ASOC

NSWC

Air support/
Reconnaissance

Combat Controllers

Pararescuemen

PROTECTING THE COUNTRY

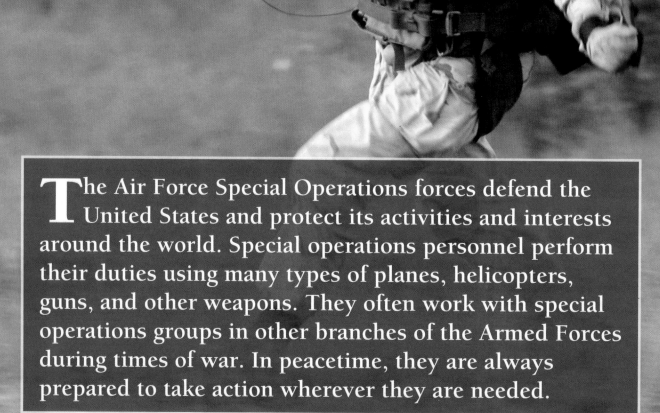

The Air Force Special Operations forces defend the United States and protect its activities and interests around the world. Special operations personnel perform their duties using many types of planes, helicopters, guns, and other weapons. They often work with special operations groups in other branches of the Armed Forces during times of war. In peacetime, they are always prepared to take action wherever they are needed.

Air Force Special Operations Command is divided into wings, groups, and squadrons. The main combat wings are the 27th and the 1st Special Operations Wings. Specialists called combat controllers manage air traffic and fight enemy forces on the ground. Pararescuemen search for, rescue, and provide medical treatment for wounded U.S. military personnel.

On the Front Lines

In times of war, Air Force Special Operations teams are mainly involved in airborne operations. They carry out specialized missions against enemy forces, including airborne attacks, reconnaissance, and search and rescue operations. Air Force Special Operations forces have taken part in U.S. military operations in many different parts of the world. They are often responsible for dropping off and picking up other U.S. special operations personnel from inside enemy territory, and providing supplies when needed.

MOTTOES

The motto of the Air Force Special Operations Command is "Any Place, Any Time, Any Where." The motto was first used by U.S. air **commandos** fighting Japanese forces in Burma during Word War II.

Combat controllers have their own motto. It is "First There." This is because they carry out dangerous missions in enemy territory and lead the way for other troops to follow.

AFSOC HISTORY

The air forces of the United States military have had special operations units ever since air warfare became a major form of battle. In World War II, the Army had responsibility for these missions. In 1947, the Air Force became an official branch of the U.S. Armed Forces. Since then, the Air Force has been in charge of specialized air operations.

1941
★ United States enters World War II

1945
★ World War II ends

1944
★ U.S. air commandos are involved in operations in Burma and in Europe

1947
★ The Air Force becomes a separate branch of the U.S. Armed Forces

1950 TO 1953
★ The Air Force organizes special operations forces in the Korean War

1965 TO 1973
★ The Air Force takes part in search and rescue missions during the Vietnam War

1944

1965

Air Force Special Operations were not under one command until 1983. That year, the Air Force created the 23rd Air Force to have responsibility for such operations. In 1990, the 23rd Air Force was renamed the Air Force Special Operations Command.

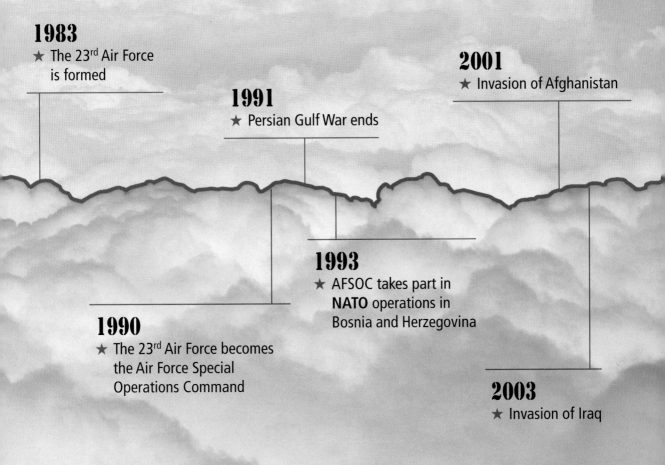

1983
★ The 23rd Air Force is formed

1991
★ Persian Gulf War ends

2001
★ Invasion of Afghanistan

1993
★ AFSOC takes part in **NATO** operations in Bosnia and Herzegovina

1990
★ The 23rd Air Force becomes the Air Force Special Operations Command

2003
★ Invasion of Iraq

2001

2003

AFSOC BASES AROUND THE WORLD

The Air Force Special Operations Command has bases with special operations teams throughout the United States. Special operations units have also been based in many countries around the world.

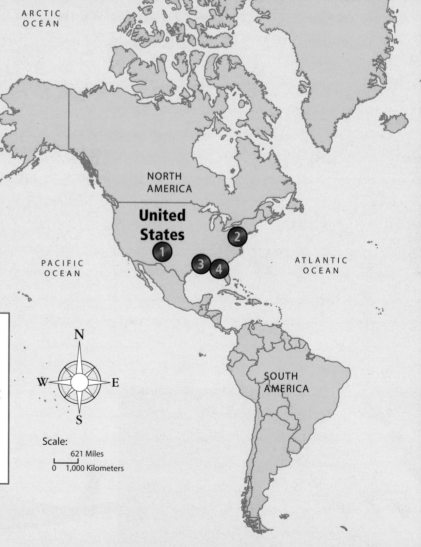

1 New Mexico

Cannon Air Force Base near Clovis is home to the 27th Special Operations Wing of AFSOC. The base has more than 2,000 personnel.

2 Pennsylvania

Harrisburg Air National Guard Base is home to the 193rd Special Operations Wing. The 193rd is part of the Pennsylvania Air National Guard, but it comes under the command of AFSOC in times of war.

Scale:
621 Miles
0   1,000 Kilometers

3 Mississippi

The Mississippi 209th Civil Engineering Squadron is based at the Air National Guard's Combat Readiness Training Center at Gulfport-Biloxi International Airport. This state National Guard squadron comes under the command of AFSOC during wartime.

4 Florida

AFSOC has its headquarters at Hurlburt Field Air Force Base in Okaloosa County. This base is part of Eglin Air Force Base, which is home to a number of other Air Force units and about 8,000 members of the U.S. Armed Forces.

5 United Kingdom

The 352nd Special Operations Group is based out of **RAF** Mildenhall. This is a Royal Air Force base in Suffolk, England. RAF Mildenhall is also the headquarters of other U.S. Air Force divisions and some units of the U.S. Navy.

6 Japan

Kadena Air Base is a major U.S. Air Force base located on the Japanese island of Okinawa. It is home to many Air Force units, including the 353rd Special Operations Group.

ARCTIC OCEAN

ASIA

EUROPE

PACIFIC OCEAN

AFRICA

INDIAN OCEAN

AUSTRALIA

AFSOC UNIFORMS

A ir Force Special Operations personnel wear different uniforms depending on their job. The battle uniform of those who fly aircraft differs from the combat uniform of those who work on the ground.

AIRMAN BATTLE UNIFORM

The Airman Battle Uniform (ABU) is similar to the Army Combat Uniform. The ABU has fewer pockets than the Army version and has a tan, gray, green, and blue **camouflage** pattern. The cap and combat boots also have this camouflage pattern. Air Force special operations personnel serving in Afghanistan wear uniforms with the MultiCam Camouflage Pattern. This consists of seven colors but looks mostly brown and greenish. It blends well with Afghanistan's landscape and with the camouflage of other U.S. military personnel serving in the country.

Pararescuemen wear a maroon beret. Combat controllers wear a bright red beret.

FLIGHT SUIT

The Air Force flight suit is made of a fireproof material called Nomex. The suits are usually green or tan in color and have multiple pockets. The flight helmet has a visor and oxygen mask, and pilots have a parachute and a life preserver for use in emergencies. They also have a survival vest that contains items such as flares, water, weapons, ammunition, knives, and medical supplies.

COMBAT UNIFORM

Air Force Special Operations personnel who work on the ground wear the Army combat uniform. The uniform is designed in the Universal Camouflage Pattern. This pattern blends tan, gray, and green to make soldiers harder to see in desert, woodland, and urban environments. The Improved Outer Tactical Vest (IOTV) can be worn over the jacket.

The helmet is made from a bullet-resistant material known as Kevlar or Twaron. A night vision device can be attached to the helmet for operations at night or in low-light environments.

The trousers are worn with a 2-inch (5-centimeter) wide nylon web belt. They have Velcro pouches and two storage pockets at both the thighs and calves. The combat boots are tan-colored. Soldiers may also wear elbow pads, kneepads, gloves, and protective eyewear.

AFSOC AIRCRAFT

AC-130 SPECTRE/ SPOOKY II GUNSHIP

The AC-130 Spectre is a cargo plane converted into a **gunship**. One side of the aircraft is equipped with different types of machine guns. It is mostly used for reconnaissance and patrolling over U.S. military forces and bases. It may also be called on to attack enemy ground forces. The plane has been used by special operations forces in the Vietnam War and in many missions since then.

CV-22 OSPREY

The CV-22 Osprey is a tilt-rotor aircraft. This means that it can take off, land, and hover like a helicopter, but can also fly like a plane. It is used to provide supplies to ground forces and to perform search and rescue missions. The aircraft can be equipped with a machine gun and other weapons. It has a crew of four and can carry up to 32 soldiers.

EC-130J COMMANDO SOLO

The EC-130J Commando Solo is a modified version of the large Hercules transport plane. The 193rd Special Operations Wing operates the Commando Solo. The aircraft is used to broadcast radio and television messages to civilians or military forces. This can provide important information to U.S. personnel and also confuse or discourage enemy forces. The aircraft can broadcast on all local radio and television channels. It carries out day and night missions and can be refueled while in the air.

MQ-1 PREDATOR

The MQ-1 Predator is an unmanned aerial vehicle (UAV). It is equipped with cameras and sensors that are linked to satellites. The vehicle can reach targets up to 400 miles (645 kilometers) away and is used mainly for reconnaissance. The Predator can also be armed with missiles to attack enemy forces.

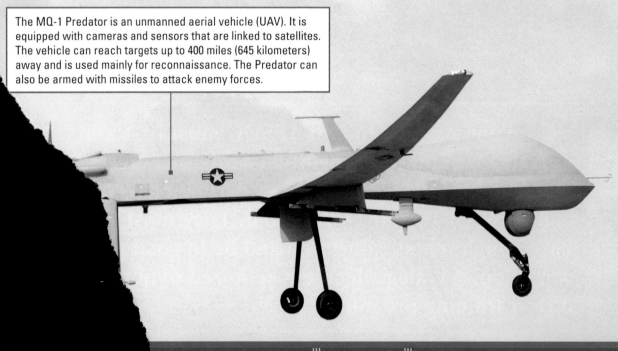

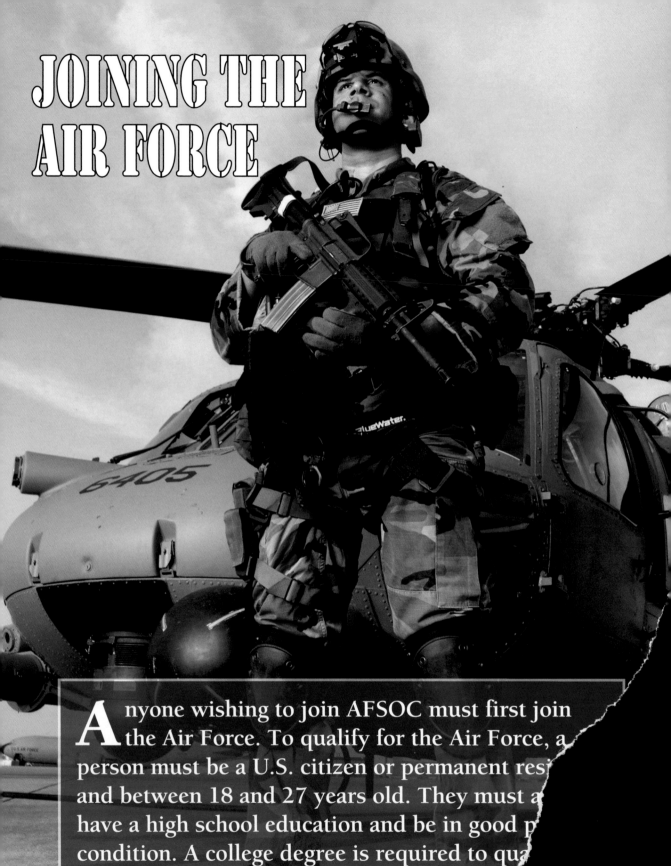

JOINING THE AIR FORCE

Anyone wishing to join AFSOC must first join the Air Force. To qualify for the Air Force, a person must be a U.S. citizen or permanent res[ident] and between 18 and 27 years old. They must a[lso] have a high school education and be in good p[hysical] condition. A college degree is required to qu[alify for] **officer** training programs.

Applying to the Air Force

Step One: Apply online

Step Two: Talk to a recruiter and ask about Air Force Special Operations teams

Step Three: Take the Armed Forces Vocational Aptitude Battery test (AFVAB)

Step Four: Visit the Military Entrance Processing Station (MEPS)

OATH OF ENLISTMENT

"I do solemnly swear that I will support and defend the Constitution of the United States against all enemies, foreign and domestic; that I will bear true faith and allegiance to the same; and that I will obey the orders of the President of the United States and the orders of the officers appointed over me, according to regulations and the Uniform Code of Military Justice. So help me God."

Boot Camp Basic training for Air Force **recruits** is sometimes called Boot Camp. It is about 8.5 weeks long. Combat controllers are among the most highly trained personnel in the U.S. Armed Forces. The first part of their training lasts for 35 weeks. Trainees learn about different types of aircraft, navigation, weather, air traffic control, communications, and radar. They also are taught basic parachuting skills and survival techniques. Special Tactics Advanced Skills Training (AST) takes ~~from~~ 12 to 15 months. It involves ~~tough~~ physical and mental training ~~and~~ advanced training in parachuting ~~and~~ scuba diving.

JOBS IN THE AIR FORCE

Being in Air Force Special Operations is not just about serving in combat. There are many careers for special operations personnel. There are jobs in communications and technology, **military intelligence**, air traffic control, electronics, and health and medicine, and jobs as weather specialists. The training and experience gained in Air Force Special Operations can also lead to successful careers in civilian life after military service is completed.

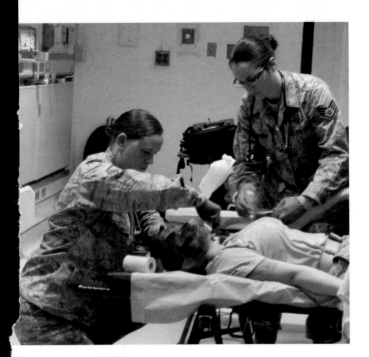

Health Care and Medicine

Special operations medical personnel take part in missions to rescue injured servicemen in enemy territory. They also provide **humanitarian services** for civilians after floods, tsunamis, earthquakes, and other natural disasters. Careers include working as doctors, nurses, laboratory researchers, and medical technicians.

Weather

Special operations weather specialists collect information about weather patterns to help in the planning of missions, both on the ground and in the air. They gather this information using radar, weather satellites, and other technology.

Communications and Technology

Jobs in this field involve working with high-tech gear, such as communications equipment and computers. Specialists in military intelligence study photographs taken by satellites or aircraft to gain information needed by all branches of the military. There are also jobs working with electronics, navigation, and radar, as well as air traffic control.

COMMUNITY LIFE

In many ways, life as Air Force Special Operations personnel is much like civilian life. They work regular hours at a job, spend time with their families, and fill their free time with hobbies, sports, and other activities. Some personnel live in barracks, but others live in houses either on or off the base.

Many bases where special operations personnel are stationed have all the facilities of most towns and cities. This may include hospitals, schools, day care centers, libraries, sports facilities, and shopping malls. Air Force Special Operations Command provides a wide variety of programs to improve the quality of life for families living on military bases. These include counseling services, programs to improve on-base education and job opportunities for family members, and programs that help families deal with the stress of having a loved one working in a combat area.

★ The reunion of special operations personnel with their families is always a joyful event.

WRITE YOUR STORY

The first step in qualifying for Air Force Special Operations is to join the Air Force. To do so, you will probably need to write an essay about yourself. This is also true when you apply to a college or for a job. Practice telling your story by completing this writing activity.

1 Brainstorming

Start by making notes about your interests. What are your hobbies? Do you like to read? Are you more interested in computers or power tools? Then, organize your ideas into an outline, with a clear beginning, middle, and end.

2 Writing the First Draft

A first draft does not have to be perfect. Try to get the story written. Then, read it to see if it makes sense. It will probably need revision. Even the most famous writers edit their work many times before it is completed.

3 Editing

Go through your story and remove anything that is repeated or not needed. Also, add any missing information that should be included. Be sure the text makes sense and is easy to read.

4 Proofreading

The proofreading stage is where you check spelling, grammar, and punctuation. You will often find mistakes that you missed during the editing stage. Always look for ways to make your writing the best it can be.

5 Submitting Your Story

When your text is finished, it is time to submit your story, along with any other application materials. A good essay will increase your chances of being accepted, whether it be for a job, a school, or the Air Force.

TEST YOUR KNOWLEDGE

1 What does AFSOC stand for?

2 What is a tilt-rotor aircraft?

3 Where is the AFSOC headquarters located?

4 What is the AFSOC motto?

5 What color beret do pararescuemen wear?

6 What are the main combat wings of the AFSOC?

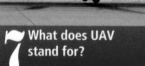

7 What does UAV stand for?

8 How many personnel are in AFSOC?

9 How long is Special Tactics Advanced Skills Training (AST)?

10 Where is the 352nd Special Operations Group based?

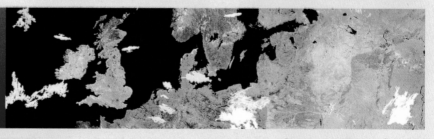

Answers: 1. Air Force Special Operations Command 2. An aircraft that can take off, hover, and land like a helicopter and also fly like a plane 3. Hurlburt Field Air Force Base in Florida 4. "Any Place, Any Time, Any Where" 5. Maroon 6. The 27th Special Operations Wing and the 1st Special Operations Wing 7. Unmanned Aerial Vehicle 8. About 15,000 9. 12 to 15 months 10. RAF Mildenhall in Suffolk, England